The Boneyard Rap
And Other Poems

Poems by Wes Magee

ustrations by Keith Brumpton

HODDER
Wayland

For Peter Wheatley
...blue sky... – W.M.

Hodder Wayland Paperback Poetry

The Upside Down Frown Collected by Andrew Fusek Peters

The Worst Class In School Collected by Brian Moses

I Wish I Could Dine With A Porcupine by Brian Moses

THE BONEYARD RAP AND
OTHER POEMS
© Hodder Wayland 2000
Text © Wes Magee 2000

Prepared for Hodder Wayland by
Mason Editorial Services
Designer: Tim Mayer

Published in 2000 by
Hodder Wayland, an imprint of
Hodder Children's Books

A Catalogue record for this book is available from
the British Library.

ISBN 0 7502 2860 1

Printed in Hong Kong

Hodder Children's Books
A division of Hodder Headline Ltd.
338 Euston Road, London NW1 3BH

CONTENTS

THE BONEYARD RAP

This is the rhythm
of the boneyard rap,
knuckle bones click
and hand bones clap,
finger bones flick
and thigh bones slap,
when you're doing the rhythm
of the boneyard rap.
      Wooooooooooooooo!

It's the boneyard rap
and it's a scare.
Give your bones a shake-up
if you dare.
Rattle your teeth
and waggle your jaw
and let's do the boneyard rap
once more.

This is the rhythm
of the boneyard rap,
elbow bones clink
and backbones snap,
shoulder bones chink
and toe bones tap,

4

when you're doing the rhythm
of the boneyard rap.
        Woooooooooooooo!

It's the boneyard rap
and it's a scare.
Give your bones a shake-up
if you dare.
Rattle your teeth
and waggle your jaw
and let's do the boneyard rap
once more.

This is the rhythm
of the boneyard rap,
ankle bones sock
and arm bones flap,
pelvic bones knock
and knee bones zap,
when you're doing the rhythm
of the boneyard rap.
        Woooooooooooooo!

PAULINE THE POLTERGEIST

At 'Creepy Cottage' something's up.
On the hall mat there's a smashed cup,
and with the ashes in the grate
lie fragments of a dinner plate.
Sharp knives and spoons are on the floor
and someone's chucked an apple core.
Who, *who's* been throwing pans and bowls?
And *who's* been flinging crusty rolls?

At midnight there's a dreadful noise
as someone hurls the children's toys.
Whizz! and Whoosh! And Clang and Crash!
Thud! and Thump! And Slam and Smash!
It's Pauline Poltergeist, a shade,
who years ago worked as a maid
and now's returned to haunt each room
and throw things with a Bash! Bang! Boom!

At 'Creepy Cottage' every day
they try to scare the ghost away
by playing tapes of 'Status Quo'
but Pauline Poltergeist won't go.
She keeps on slinging antique jugs
and lobbing snazzy coffee mugs.
Zip! and Zap! And Ping and Plop!
Maid Pauline Poltergeist won't stop.

When Pauline bunged the Christmas pud
the 'Cottage' people left for good.
They packed their bags without delay,
jumped in their Jag and sped away.
Now 'Creepy Cott.' is up for sale
but would-be buyers turn quite pale
when Pauline lets fly with a broom
and sends them squealing from the room
with a Whack! and a Wallop!
and a Zonk! Zak! Zoom!

THE GHOSTS OF 'THE GRANGE'

Miss Starvelling-Stamper died in 'twenty-four.
They found her stone-cold on the flagstoned floor.

She lay beside the kitchen's cast-iron range,
last Starvelling-Stamper to dwell at 'The Grange'.

Since then the mansion's been abandoned, locked:
its windows smashed, roof collapsed,
                                    sewers blocked.

The croquet lawn's been lost to Queen Anne's lace.
'The Grange' is now a sad, forgotten place.

EEK!

Yet, nightly, ghosts creep from each crumbling wall
and gather in the leaf-strewn marble hall

– a chambermaid drifts up the woodwormed stairs,
a skivvy flicks at cobwebs on the chairs,

two snooty butlers wait where moonbeams slant,
see there a grim and gaunt tiaraed aunt.

Miss Starvelling-Stamper's ghost – last of her line –
lifts to her lips a goblet of French wine

and floats above the kitchen's flagstoned floor
where she was found stone-cold in 'twenty-four.

In the hall. . .
cobwebs hang from the crumbling ceiling,
antlered hatstand's carved from oak,
crimson carpet's tattered and torn,
and dust in the air makes you choke.
>Chilly,
>icy mansion.
>Dank,
>deserted place.

In the kitchen. . .
tarnished taps drip brackish water,
stale loaf's grown a coat of mould,
a foul stench seeps up from the drains,
and the radiators feel stone-cold.
>Fusty,
>fetid mansion.
>Damp,
>deserted place.

On the landing. . .
a headless, rusty suit of armour,
ancient portrait's green eyes glare,
cracked mirror in a silver frame,
and rat bones on a rocking chair.
     Echoing,
       creaky mansion.
     Dark,
       deserted place.

In the bedroom. . .
a tousled bed with blood-stained pillow,
rent drapes shiver in the breeze,
cockroach scuttles over floorboards,
and a sudden shriek makes you freeze.
     Faded,
       pallid mansion.
     Dim,
       deserted place.

Up in the attic. . .
frayed dressing gowns have nests of mice,
there's Santa's sack for Christmas Eve,
a vampire bat hangs from a beam,
and the trapdoor's jammed when you try to leave. . .
     Creepy,
       scary mansion.
     Dead,
       deserted place.

Deep
down
in the darkness
of an octopus ocean,
deep
down
in the squid-ridden,
sharkery sea,
the slime beasts
are mating,
the slime beasts
are waiting
for the end of the world,
and for you,
and for me.

Deep
down
in the mudmurk
of an oyster-squashed ocean,
deep
down
in the skate-smelly,
sandsquishy sea,
the slime beasts
aren't sleeping,
the slime beasts
are creeping
to the end of the world,
and for you,
and for me.

Deep
down
in the inkpitch
of an oozeboozy ocean,
deep
down
in the seaweedy,
shipwreck-strewn sea,
the slime beasts
are slumming,
the slime beasts
are coming. . .

it's the end of the world,
and for you,
and for

me.

AT THE DEEP WELL, WHERE YOUNG JOCELYN JOAKES CLIMBED DOWN THE WINDING ROPE AND FELL TO HIS DEATH IN 1839.

Jocelyn fell
deep dark well
where

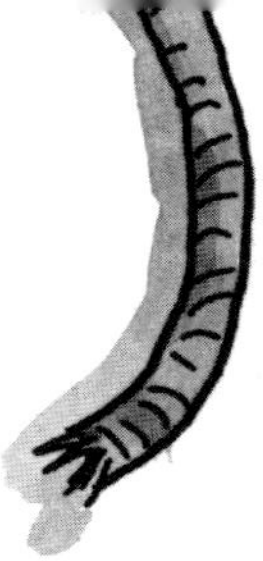

Down here lies water,
icy cold,
its secret held
from days of old.
A faint voice echoes
far below;
a boy's last cry
from years ago.

15

Here lies
Acker Abercrombie.
Crazy name,
crazy zombie.
Slightly scary,
rather rude,
he walks at midnight
in the nude.

The halves of Tracey Trump lie here.
She reached her eighty-seventh year.

She lived through floods and 2 World Wars.
Got sliced in automatic doors. . .

She never did things by halves. . .

R.I.P.
Here resteth
Werewolf
Walter Witz
who chewed relations
into bits.
Aunties, uncles, nephews,
nieces,
all ended up

Ripped In Pieces.

"Please mark my grave
with just one flower."
That was the wish of
Cynthia Tower.
So when she died
they raised a plinth
and marked upon it

"Hiya, Cynth!"

THE CHIMNEY BOY'S STORY

"Inside the chimney, high I climb.
It's dark inside the sooty stack.
I bang my head, I graze my back,
I lose all sense of passing time.
Inside the chimney,
high I climb.

"Inside the chimney, high I climb.
Far, far above. . . a patch of blue
where one white cloud drifts into view.
I stop to rest, but that's a crime.
Inside the chimney,
high I climb.

"Inside the chimney, high I climb.
My bare feet slip on crumbling bricks.
I clear rooks' nests – dead leaves and sticks.
The master yells, 'Get working, brat!'
I'm starved. Sometimes I eat stewed rat.
Soot's in my hair. I'm tasting grime.
Inside the chimney,
high I climb."

I gaze in the mirror
and my spine gives a shiver
for before my wide eyes
is a zit, zonker size
on the tip of my nose
and it's red as a rose.

I look just like a gonk
with this zit on my conk.
There's no way I'll go out
for my mates will all shout,
"What a hooter! Hey, hey!
What's this? Red Nose Day?"

When I give it a squeeze
the sharp pain makes me sneeze
and the zit explodes. Splat!
Soon the swelling's gone flat
for the zonker has split.
Problem solved. That's it, zit!

DISCO NITE

In the girls' cloakroom
the air gasps with Nightfall and Moonwind.
The excitement is intense.
Everyone uses the lip gloss
(strawberry flavoured) passed round
by Sarah Spence.

In a giggling gaggle
the girls rush to the hall
where the floor shines like a skating rink.
Loud music throbs and pounds.
The disco lights dazzle in red, mauve,
yellow, green and pink.

And *he's* there, Dean Moffat
in a big stripy shirt
and with gel on his spiky hair.
When the DJ yells,
"Go grab 'em, girls!"
Lisa drags him off his chair.

. . . .

Next morning, on the playground,
Lisa's in a huddle of girls.
"What happened?" "Tell us!" "Own up!"
Lisa smiles. "Dean loves me," she says,
"and I think he'll marry me
when we're grown-up."

OUR MISS GILL AND MR. SCOTT

Our Miss Gill and Mr. Scott
seem to like each other
rather a lot.
His her
and our class
are always going on trips together.
Today we climbed Tucker's Hill
in dreadful weather.
    "He held her hand."
        "Never!"
    "He did, and they kissed"
        "No!"
It turned terribly cold.
    "I'm freezing" said Jill.
It started to rain,
then there was sleet,
and then there was snow.

At least it was warm on the coach
and we all sang.
We arrived at the school gate
just as the bell rang.
Off we trooped home,
but at the street corner
I turned and looked back.
So did Jill,
and we watched
as our Miss Gill
crossed the car park
hand in glove
with Mr. Scott.
    "They *are* in love," said Jill.
Yes, they do seem
to like each other
rather a lot.

I like Emma
but I don't know
if she likes me.
All the boys
think I'm a fool.

I wait outside the school gate
at half-past three
trying to keep my cool.
Emma walks past,
shaking her blonde hair free,
laughs with her friends
and drifts off home for tea.

Emma's two years
older than me.
Her class is higher
up the school.

I like Emma
but I don't know
if she likes me.
All the boys
think I'm a fool.

THE CAT WITH NO NAME

In the dingy Staff Room of a school in the city,
where the teachers' damp macs hang limply from hooks,
where cracked cups are tea-stained, the worn carpet gritty,
and where there are piles of exercise books,
you will notice – at break – that the teachers don't utter
a sound: none of them grumble and none of them chat.
Why? They dare not disturb what sleeps, fat as butter,
on the Staff Room's best chair: one huge tortoiseshell cat.

For the teachers
know very well not to wake him,
for they know that he's three parts not tame.
He's a wild cat,
a wild cat,
a not-to-be-riled cat,
he's the tortoiseshell cat with no name.

It was drizzly December when the cat first appeared
and took the French teacher's chair for his bed.
Now his scimitar claws in the Staff Room are feared,
oh yes, and the street-fighter's fangs in his head.
Once a day he is seen doing arches and stretches
then for hours like a furry coiled fossil he'll lie.
It's true that he's made all the staff nervous wretches,
they approach. . . and he opens one basilisk eye.

For the teachers
know very well not to stroke him,
for they know that he'll not play the game.
He's a wild cat,
a wild cat,
a not-to-be-riled cat,
he's the tortoiseshell cat with no name.

The headmistress, the teachers and the school's cleaners
can't shift him with even a long-handled broom,
for the cat merely yawns, treats them all like has-beeners
and continues to live in that dingy Staff Room.
When the French teacher tried to reclaim her armchair
with a cat-cally, shriek-squally, "Allez-vous-en!"
The cat gave a hiss, clawed the lady's long hair
and back to Marseille Madame Touff-Pouff has gone.

For the teachers
know very well not to irk him,
for they know that he's always the same.
He's a wild cat,
a wild cat,
a not-to-be-riled cat,
he's the tortoiseshell cat with no name.

I once worked in that school and observed the huge creature's
habits as I sipped my cracked cup of weak tea.
I saw how he frightened and flummoxed the teachers
and how, every Friday, he'd one-green-eye me.
To appease him, each day we laid out a fish dinner
which the beast snaffled-up in just one minute flat,
then returned to his chair with a smirk – the old sinner!
It seems there's no way to be rid of that cat.

For the teachers
know very well not to cross him,
for they know that he's three parts not tame.
He's a wild cat,
a wild cat,
a not-to-be-riled cat

(he can't bear to be smiled at),

he's the tortoiseshell cat with no name,
with no name,
he's the tortoiseshell cat with no name.

THE DAY AFTER

I went to school
the day after dad died.
Teacher knew all about it.
She put a hand on my shoulder
        and sighed.

In class things seemed much the same
although I felt strangely subdued.
Breaktime was the same too,
and at lunchtime the usual crew
played-up the dinner supervisors.
Fraggle was downright rude.
I joined in the football game

but volunteered to go in goal.
That meant I was left almost alone,
could think things over on my own.
For once I let the others shout
        and race and roll.

. . . .

First thing that afternoon,
everyone in his and her place
for silent reading,
I suddenly felt hot tears streaming
        down my face.

Salty tears splashed down
and soaked into my book's page.
Sobs heaved in my chest.
Teacher peered over her half specs
and said quietly, "Ben, come here."
I stood at her desk, crying. At my age!
I felt like an idiot, a clown.

"Don't feel ashamed," teacher said.
"It's only right to weep.
Here, have these tissues to keep."
I dabbed my eyes, then looked around.
        Bowed into books, every head.

. . . .

"Have a cold drink.
Go with James. He'll understand."
In the boys' cloaks I drank deeply
then slowly wiped my mouth
     on the back of my hand.

Sheepishly I said, "My dad died."
"I know," said James.
"We'd best get back to class. Come on."
Walking down the corridor I thought of dad. . . gone.
In class no one sniggered,
they were busy getting changed for games.
No one noticed I'd cried.

All day I felt sad, sad.
After school I reached my street,
clutching the tissues, dragging my feet.
Mum was there in our house
     but no dad,

     no dad.

FOOTBALL! FOOTBALL!

Football! Football!
The boys want the entire playground
and we're left squashed
against the broken fence.
Why don't the teachers stop them?
　　　Why?
　　　Haven't they got *any* sense?

　　　My friend Emma
ran across the tarmac. Smack!
Got the football right on her nose.
Blood all over her face.
Why don't the teachers do something?
　　　Why?
　　　It's a disgrace, a *disgrace!*

30

Those boys. . . I mean
they're like hooligans.
CHEL-SEA! CHEL-SEA! they chant
morning, noon and night.
The teacher on duty does. . . nothing!
        Why?
        It's just. . . it's just not right!

        We complain bitterly
but the duty teacher says,
"Go and see the Head. He's in charge."
Him! He's useless! YOU-ESS-LESS!
When we ask him to ban football,
        why,
        oh why, can't he just say, "Yes"?

red!

OH, NO YOU DON'T!

For a Christmas treat
dad took me and four friends
to see 'Cinderella' in town.
There was loud music, excitement
and sweets in crackly paper
when the theatre lights went down.

During the interval
we put away choc ices
and bottles of fizzy drink.
Then, on stage, mice and a pumpkin
became coach and horses
quicker than you could blink.

Now, wearing day-glo wigs,
the Ugly Sisters waddled on.
Their noses were painted blue.

"Oh, no you don't!" they screeched.
"Oh, yes we do!" "Oh, no you don't!"
"OH, YES WE DO! OH, YES WE DO!"

When it was over we filed out
and squashed into the back seat
of dad's old car.
Jolting, we headed home.
"Look, the Moon!" "There's the Plough!"
"And the North Star!"

Suddenly, Samantha said,
"Emma looks ill.
I think she's going to be sick."
"Oh, no she isn't," dad muttered grimly.
"Oh, yes she is!" we chorused.
"Stop the car. Quick! QUICK!"

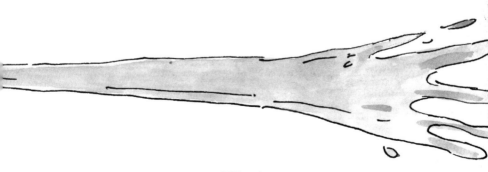

WHOOSH! CHEETAH!

A member of the Cat family
     and sucH a speedy sprintah.
          It racEs across Africa's plains
     to catch antelopE and zebrah.
          Can climb a Tree with agilitee,
               and is All quicksilver speed. A dashah!
Whoosh! CheetaH!

TIGER NIGHT

Tiger,
a creature of contrasts.

Here, just demanding to be stroked,
the velvety-soft, striped fur coat.

There, one huge raised paw,
that can strike dead gazelle, gnu or goat.

Tiger,
a creature of contrasts.

Here, the glinting eyes,
pools of shifting light. Tiger bright.

There, the watchful beast, tense,
lurking in shadows. Tiger fear. Tiger might.

GUARD WOLF IN SIBERIA

My coat is thick,
my teeth are strong.
The snow lies deep,
the winter's long.

I stand on guard
here in the cold.
The pack's asleep.
Some grow old.
I live by hunting,
men hunt me.
When guns spit fire
we run, we flee.

My coat is thick,
my teeth are strong.
The snow lies deep,
the winter's long.

In fairy tales
I roamed the wood,
the bad wolf in
'Red Riding Hood'.
If I howl now
the pack will wake.
We'll flee across
the frozen lake.

My coat is thick,
my teeth are strong.
The snow lies deep,
the winter's long.

Not
a
twig
stirs.
The frost-bitten garden
huddles beneath
a heaped duvet of snow.
Pond,
tree,
sky
and
street
are granite with cold.

WHAT IS. . . THE BEAST WITH NO NAME?
(A RIDDLE)

Vaster than a galaxy
     the Beast with No Name
slithers along the spaceways
sucking into its dark stomach
dead comets, meteorites
and abandoned space probes.

With a single nudge
     the Beast with No Name
sets the planets spinning.
Its face has never been seen.
The Beast is the colour of darkness
and its journey across the universe is endless.

At dusk you can watch
     the Beast with No Name
blot out the sun as it passes by.
Those are not stars you see
but a billion burning spots
which itch wickedly on its thick skin.

" . . . Errr. . . Tickets, please. Mr. Beast. . . "

38

Answer on page 48.

Take a sheet of paper
and fold it.
Fold it again, and again, and again.
By the 6th fold
it is 1 centimetre thick. Yes?

By the 11th fold
it will be 32 centimetres thick,
and by the 15th fold
– 5 metres.

At the 24th fold
it is 2.5 kilometres,
and by fold 30
measures 160 kilometres high.

At the 35th fold
– 5,000 kilometres.
At the 43rd fold
it will reach to the Moon.

And by fold 52
it will stretch
from here
. . . to the Sun.

Take a sheet of paper.
Go on.   Try it!

THE TRAVELLIN' BRITAIN RAP

All the drivers rattlin' on
in a million fast cars
drivin' up and down the country
like motor racin' stars,
on clearway,
    motorway,
        carriageway
           and street,
then roundabout and road
through rain and hail and sleet,
drivin' up and down the country
till they're feelin' dead beat,
and the
    traffic noise
        traffic noise
           has turned them half deaf
so they take a welcome break
at Happy Eater, Little Chef

   and

     then

       they're

drivin' on, drivin' on
as the tyres zip and zap
through a thousand towns and cities
that are dotted on the map,
at least a million cars
– British, German, French and Jap,
    never stopping'
        country hoppin'
            never stoppin'
                country hoppin'
for all the cars are movin'
to the travellin' Britain rap,
for all the cars are movin'
to the travellin' Britain rap,
for all the cars are movin'
to

    the

        travellin'

            Britain

                rap!

                    YEAH!

REMEMBERING DINOSAURS

Years ago, on a drizzly day,
my uncle drove me across Dorset
       until we arrived at
an abandoned quarry near Lyme Regis.
"Just the day for dinosaurs," he quipped
       as I lugged on wellies, coat and hat.

Plodding through that muddy moonscape
we found fossilized footprints
       stomped by dinosaurs epochs ago.
"Stegosaurus walked this way!" uncle joked
as he waddled along the path
chortling like a half-crazed crow.

Further on we spotted petrified eggs,
exposed, and big as footballs.
    Uncle cracked, "Boil me two for breks!"
and made me grin that grey day.
Overhead, thunder bellowed and boomed.
        "Hey up! Here's tyrannosaurus rex!"

Years ago, yet I remember that visit
and the dinosaur names he taught me
        – diplodocus, triceratops, dimetrodon.
He made a damp day bright,
remains stamped on my memory
        even though, like the dinosaurs,
            he's long, long gone.

NOISY AND QUIET PLACES

In York
they squawk.
In Leek
they shriek.
In Dore
they roar.
On Skye
they cry.
Yet in Llanfairgwyn-thisper-and-thistle
they just, er,
whisper and whistle.

In Stoke
they croak.
In Fleet
they bleat.
In Diss
they hiss.
In Sale
they wail.
Yet in Llanfairgwyn-stumble-and-stutter
they just, er,
mumble and mutter.

In Tring
they sing.
In Stone
they moan.
In Birse
they curse.
In Stroud
they're loud.
Yet in Llanfairgwyn-gruffle-and-griffle
they just, er,
snuffle and sniffle.

Faraway places
are calling to me,
calling to me
over land, over sea.
Snow-mufflered Moscow,
the frozen South Pole,
east to Kyoto,
Hong Kong and Seoul.
Dripping wet jungles,
vast African plain,
north to Yakutsk
by Siberian train.
Matterhorn mountain,
drift on the Med.
Nights in the desert
with stars overhead.
Outer Mongolia,
Isle of Magee,
faraway places
are calling to me.
Grand Coulee Dam,
Belize and Bel-Air,
Kabul, Kurdistan,
and County Kildare.

Faraway places
are calling to me,
calling to me
over land, over sea.
Faraway places
are calling me there,
the sun on my face,
the wind in my hair.
Faraway places
are calling me,
calling me,
calling me there.

SUN

Thermonuclear heart
you throb at the centre
of the Solar System,
our giver of warmth,
light.

Your atomic blaze of energy
seems endless, infinite.
At evening you are crimson-faced:
in high summer – blinding
white.

Golden mouth, thirstily you gulp
puddle, pool, pond and river.
Kindly you warm the cold Moon
on a freezing December
night.

Burning bonfire of the skies,
we bask in your beams.
Always be there, Sun, always rise,
ever glowing, gleaming
bright.

HUMPBACK WHALE

Our living island,
your sad song echoes
beneath the icebergs.

Survive and swim free
in the cold oceans,
our living island.

MORE POETRY FROM HODDER WAYLAND

Hodder Wayland Poetry Collections:
Themed anthologies illustrated by Kelly Waldek.
270 x 220 mm, full-colour, 32 pages: £9.99 hb/£4.99 pb

Poems About Animals
Poems About Festivals
Poems About Food

Poems About Seasons
Poems About Space
Poems About School

Poems About Me/Poems About You and Me:
Poetry about what it means to be a member of society.
270 x 220 mm, full-colour, 32 pages: £9.50 hb/£4.99 pb

Also available as big books/educational packs
Big Books 440 x 360 mm, £13.99

The Upside Down Frown: Shape poems
With illustrations by Mike Flanagan. Andrew Fusek Peters
has collected a selection of poems that will make you think
again about poetry, featuring worms that actually turn, a girl
who sneezes mushy peas, and many more weirdnesses besides.
204 x 145mm, black and white, 48 pages, £3.99 pb only

I Wish I Could Dine With A Porcupine
With illustrations by Kelly Waldek. A Bigfoot in the house, taking a pet iguana for a
walk and a trip to the aquarium, among other things, all come alive in the poems of
Brian Moses. *204 x 145mm, black and white, 48 pages, £4.50 pb only*

Poems About:
Themed collections of poems for primary
children with full-colour photographs.
*270 x 220 mm full-colour, £4.99
pb only*

Poems About Families
Poems About Feelings
Poems About Journeys
Poems About Weather

TO ORDER
Contact Hodder
Wayland's Customer
Services Department on:
01235 400414,
or write to them at:
39 Milton Park,
Abingdon,
Oxon OX10 4TD, UK

Page 38 answer: the night